# Using iPads® and Other Cutting-Edge Technology to Strengthen Your Instruction

*Best Apps and Technology to Engage ALL Students and Increase Learning: High Achievers, Special Needs, English Language Learners, and More!*

Fitzell, Susan Gingras
Strengthen Your Instruction Using iPads® and Other
Cutting-Edge Technology with Your Students with
Special Needs: Best Apps and Technology to Engage ALL Students and Increase
Learning (Grades 6-12)
ISBN: 1932995250

For information, contact:
Susan Gingras Fitzell, M.Ed. CSP
Cogent Catalyst Publications
PO Box 6182
Manchester, NH 03108-6182
603-625-6087

Email:
info@cogentcatalyst.com
SFitzell@SusanFitzell.com

Other selected titles by Susan Gingras Fitzell, M.Ed.
- Co-Teaching and Collaboration in the General Classroom
- Paraprofessionals and Teachers Working Together
- Special Needs in the General Classroom: Strategies That Make it Work
- RTI for Secondary Teachers
- Free the Children: Conflict Education for Strong Peaceful Minds
- Transforming Anger to Personal Power: An Anger Management Curriculum Guide for Grades 6 through 12
- Umm... Studying? What's That? Learning Strategies for the Overwhelmed and Confused College and High School Student
- Please Help Me With My Homework: Strategies for Parents and Caregivers
- Memorization and Test Taking Strategies (DVD Professional Development)

# Introduction

Bonding opportunities with a 22-year-old son are few and far between, especially when what your son thinks is exciting is not your idea of a good time. However, I'm at a stage in life where I've decided the benefit to myself professionally, as well as personally, for stepping out of my comfort zone is worth the risk and effort. In January of 2012 my son asked me to go skydiving with him. I told him he was out of his mind. There was absolutely no way that I was jumping out of a perfectly good airplane. However, in the months that followed, a series of events came together which included a terrific discount coupon for a skydiving adventure, so I decided to take the leap and enjoy this bonding experience with my son. I stepped way out of my comfort zone.

What does that have to do with this seminar and this book? I have never considered myself a technology guru. I am a teacher who loves practical solutions that work to promote student success. I also value efficiency and respect the challenges that teachers face in a job overloaded with high expectations and sometimes ridiculous demands. When I was asked to put together a seminar on iPad apps for secondary students, I balked. Out of my comfort zone. I didn't even own an iPad. However, I have committed myself to growth and this year that meant doing things that were uncomfortable, new, challenging, and time-consuming. As an educational consultant, teacher, and mother to a college student with a learning disability, I need to grow my skills so that I could provide solutions to the learning challenges that others face.

As I approached the task of pulling together and learning about iPad apps, Android apps, portable apps, and websites, I realized that I could not do what I have seen many other presenters and webinar providers do. What is that? Create a book or presentation of hundreds of apps that look great on the surface, but have not been tested with real life applications. There are thousands of apps out there. Of those thousands, thousands are not worth your time or money.

Consequently, my approach to this challenge has been to download, test, and try iPad apps, portable apps, and a few apps that are cross-platform so that I could provide you with solutions that work and don't waste your time, or your students' time. In the process, I will share some of the realities of shopping for apps, show you apps that work well, and tell you why I like certain apps and why I don't like others.

So, you want to get hundreds of apps in this book and seminar. Personally, I believe that would be a waste of paper and time. Those same apps can be found in the iTunes Store, Google Play, and online. You do not need me to list them here. Consider what I present to be a beginning. Another reality that we face is that as I write this book, months before it goes into publication for the seminar you may be attending, many of these apps will have changed. Consequently, there is space available for you to take notes and add new information about apps, websites, and programs that I might find after I send this book to the publisher.

I challenge you to step out of your comfort zone and try some of these tools in your classroom or with your own child. For many students, this could make or break their success in school. I would like you to know that, at this very moment, what you are reading was not typed or written longhand in its first draft. Rather than typing or writing I am speaking what you are reading into Dragon Speak Professional, a voice to text program. I have used this program to write two other books in their first iteration. After I have a draft spoken, I work with an editor and a proofreader and massage the text into a manuscript, which is finally delivered to the publisher.

I challenge you to let go of long-held beliefs about how students must perform and show their knowledge and understanding. Brilliance need not require excellent writing skills to shine forth. Brilliance can present itself through multiple modes of communication. When we dismiss a child's brilliance because they cannot show what they know in a traditional education setting, for them, we deny the world that child's gifts.

So let's get started and see what technology can do for us and our youth.

# Chapter 1 – Why Incorporate Apps in Your Classroom

## Before We Begin...

Apps list not exhaustive-just a sample of what is available

iDevices and Apps for Assistive Technology and/or AAC (Communication) should be considered in conjunction with an evaluation by a qualified specialist as part of a comprehensive plan

## App and Device Management

### Education:

Can use a cart for updating, loading apps en masse (PowerSync Cart, http://apple.bretford.com/products/ )
App licensing for education available
(http://www.apple.com/itunes/education/ )
Do NOT need to have credit card "on file" in iTunes to have an account

### Personal:

Must have your iTunes account on device to update or add apps
Can have multiple accounts on one device, but can only sync to one computer, or lose the apps from the other account
Up to five devices for personal use per app

Recommend: Once a week updating for devices/apps!

## iTunes and Dropbox:

I just spent an entire week figuring out how to store iTunes in Dropbox. I do pay for the 200 GB account in Dropbox, which makes storing my iTunes library there possible.  I am going to list some articles on the web that share instructions on how to use Dropbox for your iTunes library. However, here are a few additional tips.

First and most important - back up your iTunes library! That means making sure every single song and movie that you have in your iTunes library is stored in a single place on your computer or on a hard drive that you can access to restore any losses you might incur in the process of moving your library to Dropbox and syncing it with multiple computers.

Secondly, sync one computer at a time. Make sure that Dropbox on other computers is not syncing. Look at the taskbar on your computer that shows what programs are running and exit out of Dropbox. That way, if something gets messed up in the process you won't have to deal with the same problem on all of your computers or devices.

At one point, I deleted my libraries from both hard drives and then went on the web and deleted it there too. Then, I copied my complete, backed up, iTunes library folder into Dropbox and walked away so that it would sink on the web. I only had one box open on one computer. Once that was done, and one computer was set, then I synced the other computer so that the libraries were exactly the same. Using Dropbox for iTunes can make tremendous sense if you use multiple computers, however it can be a nightmare if you're not careful in the implementation. Read the following articles before attempting this task.

http://www.macstories.net/tutorials/how-to-sync-your-entire-itunes-library-with-dropbox/

http://www.macstories.net/tutorials/how-to-sync-your-entire-itunes-library-with-dropbox/

## Apps that are Included on your iPad

There may be additional apps by the time this seminar takes place. Some new social networking apps loaded with the latest iOS update the week this book went to print. The apps currently included are:

- Calendar with Alerts (if desired)
- Contacts
- Photos (picture library)
- Camera
- Voice Memo
- Notes
- Clock
- iTunes
- iPod (music library)
- Safari
- App Store
- Game Center
- You Tube
- Maps
- Mail
- Face Time (iPad 2 and iPod Touch)

Dropbox can be used by students to view/download their textbooks and other course content.

The free version of Dropbox includes 2GB of file storage, which should be more than enough for most classes or courses. If you exceed the free storage limit, then you'll need to upgrade to a paid account. It is also important to note that shared files and folders count toward all users' storage limits. So plan what you share, and who you share it with, carefully.

## Dropbox

Dropbox is a free service that lets you access your photos, docs, and videos anywhere. Any file you save to your Dropbox is accessible from all your computers, iPhone, iPad and even the Dropbox website!

With this accessibility app you can take your work on the go and review docs when you're out and about.

Note: Just as any file you add will be accessible from all of your computers, any file you delete will be deleted from all of your devices. It is not a good idea to "drag and drop" files when working with Dropbox. Instead, always copy and paste your files.

Price: Free

We live in a digital era. In fact, we've been living in a digital era for quite some time now. Students are very familiar and very comfortable with all that the digital era contains because technology is all around them – oftentimes it consumes them.

Students are native speakers of the language of computers, video games and the Internet. So why not incorporate them into the classroom through the use of apps? Why not meld the world of technology with the world of education?

*For households in the United States with children 8 years old or younger:

Television adoption is almost universal - 98% have a television in the home

72% of children have access to a computer at home

67% of children own a video game system (24% own a portable video game system)

29% of children own an educational gaming system

42% of children have a television in their bedroom

2% of children own a cell phone

29% of children have a video player in their bedroom

11% of children have a video game system in their bedroom

4% of children have a computer in their bedroom

68% of households have cable TV

80% of households have a video player

68% of households have highspeed internet

9% of households have an e-reader

*Source: http://www.techaddiction.ca/children-and-technology.html

# Chapter 2 – How to Get Started

So what are apps and what makes them useful in the classroom? Apps are basically computer applications designed for mobile devices like smartphones or, more particularly, iPads.

The first thing you need to understand about iPad apps is how to actually use the iPad, and then how to utilize the right apps for your classroom. Keep in mind that your students know more about this 7" by 9" piece of metal weighing less than two pounds, but packing a very big punch, than you do. They are neither intimidated by it, nor are they scared of taking risks with it. You must be of this mindset as well.

The following diagrams are of an iPad and its features. These features are the basic building blocks you will need to understand when using an iPad.

To build your confidence in using the iPad, there are many tutorials, or user guides, available to assist you. In fact, you can find a user guide directly on your iPad by accessing Safari from your iPad toolbar, then the Bookmarks icon, then scroll down to the icon on the bottom that reads, "iPad User Guide."

## Features of the Operating System

- Voice Over
- Zoom
- Restrictions
- Auto-Correction, Auto-Capitalization
- International Keyboards
- Font Size
- White on Black

# Overview

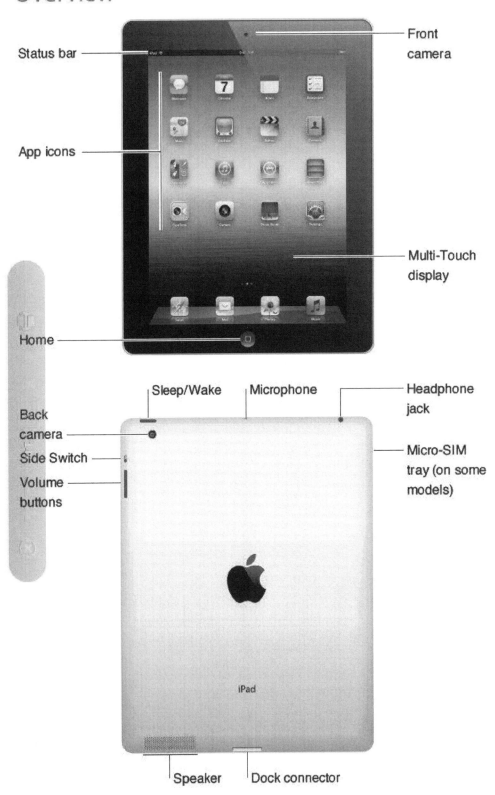

Status bar

App icons

Home

Front camera

Multi-Touch display

Sleep/Wake    Microphone

Back camera

Side Switch

Volume buttons

Headphone jack

Micro-SIM tray (on some models)

iPad

Speaker    Dock connector

## How to take a Screenshot

Press and release the Sleep/Wake button and the Home button at the same time. The screenshot is added to your Camera Roll album.
Note: On an iPad without a camera, screenshots are added to the Saved Photos album.

If your Android device is using Android version 4.0 or later, hold down the Volume Down and Power buttons at the same time to take a screenshot. For earlier versions of Android, you will need to download an app from the Google Play store. There are several good apps available.

## Greenshot

This app is a PC screenshot software tool. If you are creating screenshots to use in another program or project, this app is the right tool for you. It simplifies creation, and it is easy to understand. You and/or your students can use this app to take screenshots and input them into other programs.

Price: Free (it is a downloadable program for both Mac and PC.)

# Chapter 3 - Organization

We're all familiar with the quote, "A place for everything, and everything in its place." Well, for teachers that is the story of our lives in the classroom. Being organized always helps you to be more efficient so, when incorporating the use of iPads in your classroom, it's beneficial to keep your apps organized. You're already learning to use it, so why not avoid the stress of having your apps scattered everywhere, or having apps on your iPad that you don't use that are just taking up space? Creating folders for your apps, being able to move your apps around, and delete them when you need to, will be instrumental in staying organized.

## To move an app

Hold down on the app icon for a few seconds until it and all of the apps on the screen start to "shake." Now, move the app up/down, left/right on the screen to move it. If you want to change the Page of the app, bring it to the center of the Page left/right and it will "move" to the proper spot.

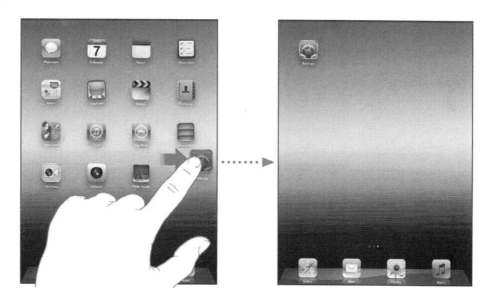

## To delete an app

Simply hold it down like before and the apps will begin to shake again. You'll see a small "X" appear on the top right of the app. Click on the "X" to delete the app from your iPad.

## To shut off the iPad

Shutting off the iPad is just a matter of holding down the On/Off Button at the top and sliding the white/red arrow to the right.

## To add web shortcuts to your Page

To add web short cuts on your Page Screen or Home Page open up the Safari web browser to a web page, click on the turning arrow button and scroll down the menu to the "Add to Home Screen" button.

## Create folders:

http://www.youtube.com/watch?v=W2p0h7q00jw

# Chapter 4 - Accessibility

## Accessibility Options

Many students with special needs, learning disabilities, or attention issues can benefit from the accessibility options already in place on the iPad.

I use some of them just because they make sense. Increasing font size and voice to text are good ways to use the iPad to increase productivity and efficiency.

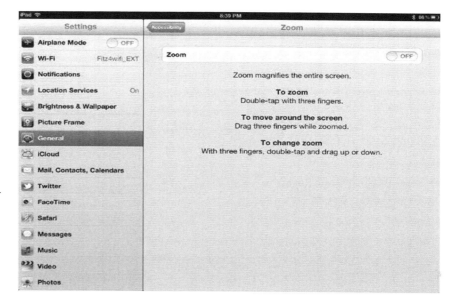

As you continue to acclimate yourself to your iPad you will notice other tools that will help you feel more comfortable using it.

These tools are included under the 'Settings' icon where you can zoom the screen or increase the text font size...

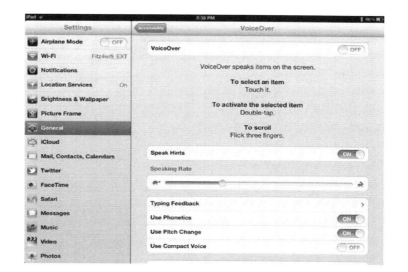

Zoom or magnify the text...

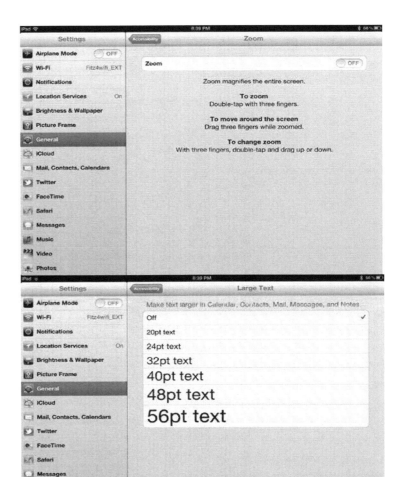

Increase the font size...

## The Text-to-Speech function

This function is built into the iOS.
It allows text from Notes, web pages,
and books to be read digitally.

## Voice Over:

http://www.dummies.com/how-to/content/for-seniors-add-voiceover-to-ipad-2.html

I do not find the voice over feature on the iPad to be easy to use. I found the above article as a reference to support your use of voiceover. However, I believe it will take some time for the user to become familiar with the differences and how one must operate the iPad with voiceover activated.

For a YouTube Video on Voice Over:
http://www.youtube.com/watch?v=4AYmFGYZkxA

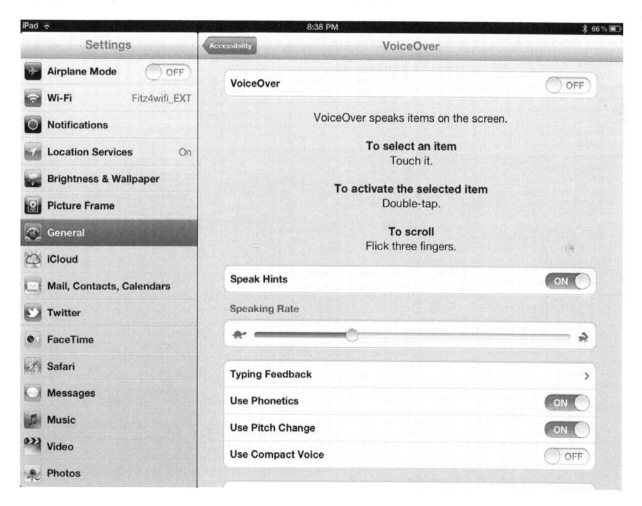

Beyond what is internal to the iPad, there are apps available, either for free or for a fee, that will provide accommodations and adapt material to meet IEP requirements and goals. Some of these apps are useful, while some are not worth your time.

*The Magnifying Glass app is one such app that is NOT worth your time.*

My hope is that eventually, these types of apps are of a better quality.

Price: Free

I also don't have time for *Free* apps that provide minimal functionality before asking me for money.

Overall, the more you familiarize yourself with the features and functions of the iPad, the more confident you will feel when you begin using apps in your classroom teaching.

## Magnifying Glass

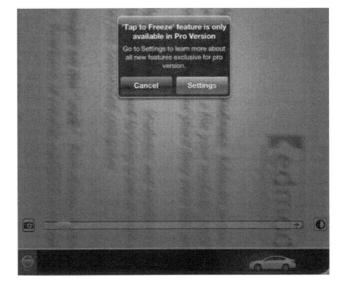

## Magnify - Android

This app uses the camera to magnify whatever your looking at.

Magnify wins the review wars in the Google Play store.

There are apps available to help those with visual and hearing challenges in addition to those with different learning styles.

### Sign Smith ASL

Teach students to finger spell their vocabulary and spelling words using sign language. Not only will they learn vocabulary, they'll learn a great skill at the same time. Hand out copies of the sign alphabet and ask students to learn to finger-spell a few vocabulary words for homework.

In class, have students pair up and teach each other the words they learned. Not only will they learn to spell those words, they will gain a life skill in the process!

Price: $4.99

ASL American Sign Language: a flashcard program that shows how to sign the alphabet.

Price: Free

## Proloquo2Go

This app gives speech-impaired children a voice. Proloquo2Go® is a communication solution for people who have difficulty speaking. It provides natural sounding text-to-speech voices in English.

It comes preloaded with lots of categories like: emotions, foods, animals, sports, hobbies, etc.,. You can add/create sentences from these categories to support speech development.

Proloquo2Go is the only app that provides genuine American and British children's voices.

Price: $189.99

## Assistive Chat

It has been called the "Best expressive language app" and it caters to people with speech difficulties. Assistive Chat has landscape and portrait modes and is designed to be simple and efficient, allowing users to communicate at the fastest rate possible, with natural sounding voices.

Price: $24.99

Teachers with students who have autism will find this app very useful because students can hear the correct pronunciation of words as they type them.

## Sono Flex Lite

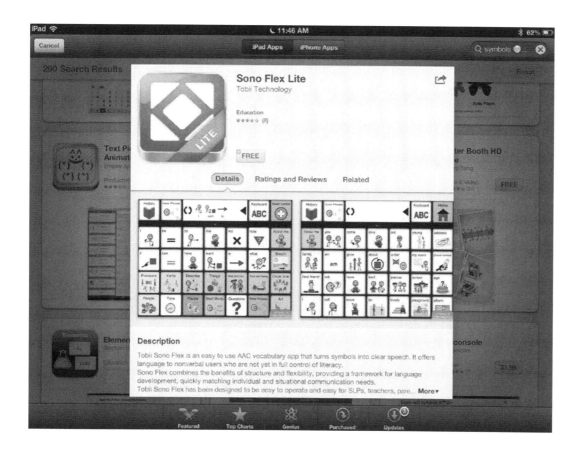

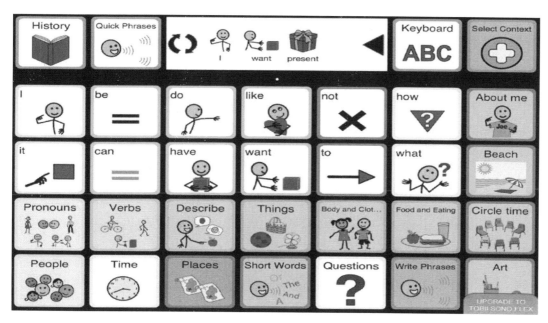

This is the first app that I have found that allows you to use a free version that actually works for Rebus writing. You can create a sentence by touching the pictures and adding them to that rectangular box at the top of screen. Once you add the newly created sentence to the history you can then touch that sentence picture string and the app will read the sentence to you.

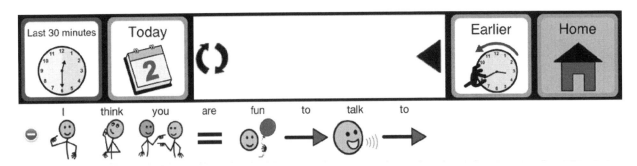

I found an app that is literally transformed how I do my slides in my presentations. I'm really aiming for less is more, as well as a clean look. The app is called haiku — and what is absolutely fantastic about it is that it is free and that means truly free. They make their money by selling additional presentation styles and scenes. However, if you're happy using the choices presented in the free app you can do whole lot for no extra cost. I absolutely love this app. I create a slide. Then I played the slide until the main menu command disappears from the top of the screen. Then I take a screenshot of my iPad and save the slide to my camera roll. I upload the camera roll slide using dropbox to my desktop. Now I can use the slide in my presentation as a picture. If this sounds complicated, it's not. It's incredibly easy and the results are gorgeous.

| | |
|---|---|
| **Typ-O**<br> | Not just word prediction! Typ-O knows how you misspell words. This is how it finds the right words for even your worst typos.<br><br>Need confirmation? Just press play! Typ-O will read the suggested words aloud for you, as well as the text you have already typed.<br><br>Typ-O is easy to use, and puts world-class word prediction and spelling error modelling at your fingertips.<br><br>Price: $14.99 |

## Scene Speak

Scene Speak is a versatile and customizable app. On the iPad, it creates interactive visual scene displays and social stories. It is a wonderful communication tool for those with Autism, Aphasia, Apraxia, developmental disabilities, or anyone wanting to enhance receptive language or visual memory.

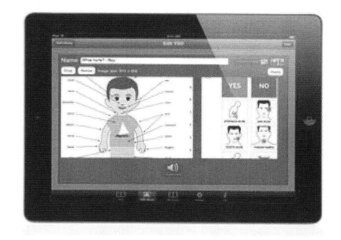

You can add custom images and download them from another computer, record your voice, create social stories, and even share your files with others. This app helps to improve and, even better, develop the language and visual memory of students with learning difficulties.

Price: $9.99

## Pocket Picture Planner HD

This is an ideal self-management app for children, users with autism and other cognitive disabilities. It lets you view a personalized visual calendar of scheduled activities created with the desktop software, Picture Planner.

Available ONLY for iOS devices.

Says it's free in the store but it is actually $199.00 to get past the demo version

While this app is expensive, it can be a very useful app for those who need this type of support.

Price: $199.99 (The "free" demo version only let's you see what the program can do.).

## Timer Apps

The most effective time managers, of the teachers that I've observed, are those that use visual timers for everything that they do in the classroom. These teachers also chunk their lesson plans, designating specific minutes to introduce material or practice material and reach different learning styles.

Keep students on task during activities. Use visual timers during class activities such as think-pair-shares, group work, timed individual assignments, etc. A visual timer is one that enables students to "see" time.

### On-Screen Timer to Keep Kids on Track!

During a recent seminar, Brenda expressed a need for an on-screen timer; something that she could put on the desktop to "signal students that their time is up." We did a little research and found a solution to help you too!

### Interval Timer - Seconds

Amazing functionality, though it may be too complex for some classroom use.

Price: Free

### Timer+ Touch HD

 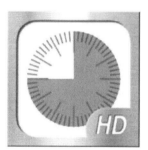

This is my favorite iPad timer App. It's so easy to use. Touch the app and move your fingers in clockwise direction to set time. Timer is shown in different colors for
- Minutes in RED
- Hours in BLUE
- Seconds in GREEN

Price: $0.99

T

## PC Chrono

PC Chrono has a timer, alarm, stopwatch, and countdown timer. It is an all-in-one program that is easy to configure and navigate through. It is a very basic, free app that comes with limited features; no sound settings.

You will need to be online to use the browser app at Online-Stopwatch.com. It has a variety of different timer options but you have to have an internet connection and your computer must be flash-enabled in order for you to use it.

Both PC Chrono and Online-Stopwatch are free.

## Online-Stopwatch

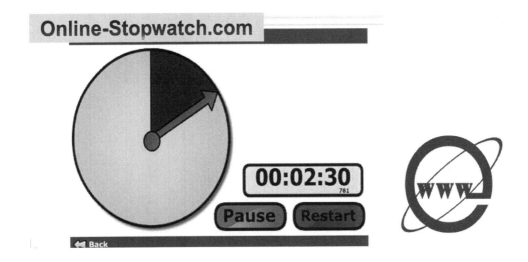

Also...

Use instrumental music clips or cell phone ring tones as timers: Sort them by how long they take to play and use them as auditory timers for students during transitions or non-reading activities - the music will cue students in to the 'time' and keep them hopping. Avoid playing music while students are reading.

**Hybrid Stopwatch and Timer**

Stopwatch and countdown timer with analog/digital display.

Price: Free

## More Timers

**Clock:** Great app for seeing what time it is in many parts of the world. It's called Clock, but it's truly a WORLD Clock It includes an alarm, stopwatch and timer.

**Sand Timer:** Easy to use. Must put up with advertisement at the bottom of the screen. Cool digital and graphic visual.

**Alarm Clock HD Free:** Was only available for iPhone when I wrote the original handbook. Now it is available for iPad. This alarm is completely digital and provides the weather. Given the other options available, I would only use this as a digital alarm for the bedroom.

Clock          Sand Timer          Alarm Clock          Night Stand

## *Bright Ideas*

# Chapter 5 - Notetaking

The iPad provides app choices for notetaking:
- Audio
- Handwriting/Drawing
- Text Input

## AudioNote

Works like the LiveScribe pen. It can type or write text while recording, then play back notes with audio tagged to the notes. It will record as a student types and play back from specific words. The key is that the student MUST be within 10 feet of the voice speaker.

Price: $4.99

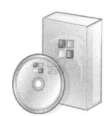

## FieldNotesLT

A note taking tool for iPhone/iPad to take with you on the road: locate your position using GPS and view a satellite map of the location, take notes, or collect photographs. Then transmit this information via e-mail.

Price: Free

## iNote

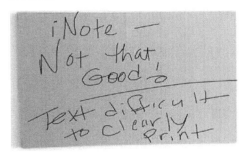

Not worth your time.

## PenUltimate

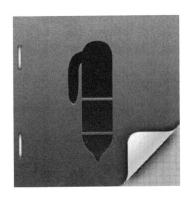

Penultimate writes and prints better than all the other writing apps I tried. However, it does not orient to landscape mode and is limited in it's capability given what one can do with the other apps.

Price: $0.99

**FreeNote, note everything**
A do anything note-taker. There are many different modes and styles available, from typing to handwriting and painting. It also has voice and video input options, a calendar and alarm. It does the work of three or four iPad apps. My 22 year old son is using it in engineering school and loves it.  Price: Free

**ColorNote**
A simple notepad app. Write notes, memos, and to-do lists.

Price: Free

## Notability

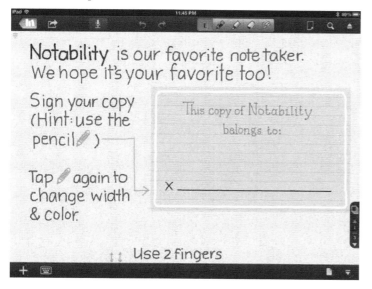

A note-taking app that is very popular and user –friendly. It includes a user guide to help you learn the app. It is a simple-looking app without a lot of visual images, but works very efficiently.

One of the things I liked about Notability's user guide is that it is short, clear, and to the point (about three pages).

A key feature is the ability to annotate on top of the content you have just added.

*Simply Googling a term such as "Best Note-Taking Apps for iPad" will take you to reviews from legitimate sources such as Gizmodo, Life Hacker, PC Magazine, etc.

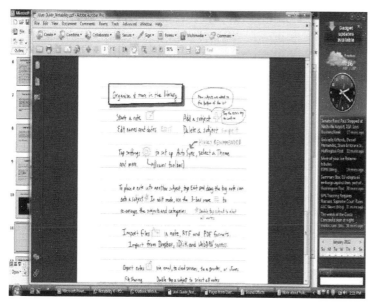

It's great to use in the classroom to create tests or class notes and add to them directly from the screen as you're presenting the notes to the class.

Type "Notability" in the YouTube search box for all kinds of "how to" videos.

Price: $0.99 (and well worth the price.)

## PDF-Notes for iPad

PDF-Notes is an essential app for your iPad device that allows you to easily manage all your PDF files. The app offers the best finger writing experience with various pens, erasers, and highlighters. The user can easily import or export any PDF file via email, Dropbox, Safari, or iTunes.

It is a great app for both annotating a PDF file and writing simple notes. You can also save and share your files with others.

Price: $9.99

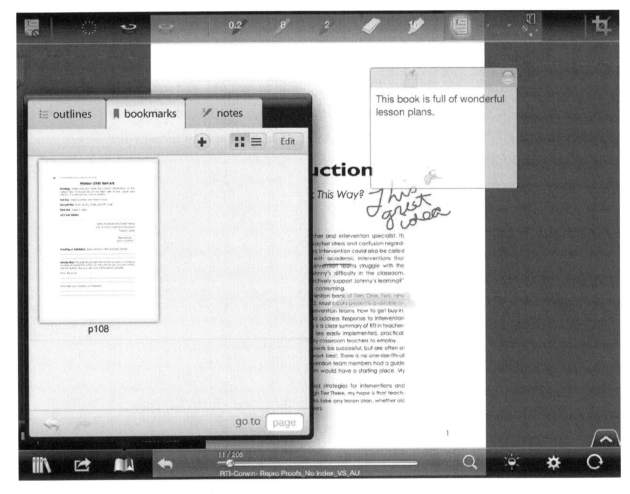

## ezPDF Reader
## PDF Annotate Form

This app trumps PDF-Notes for iPad. It is a PDF viewer, annotator, and form filler.

Price: $3.25

## qPDF Notes Demo – Reader, Form

An all-in-one PDF editing app to markup/annotate, fill/submit forms, and digitally sign PDF documents.

Price: Free (Pro version available)

## Siri Dictation App

The new iPad:
Dictation
(And Privacy Concerns)

*Why Does The New iPad's Dictation Feature Require A Wi-Fi Connection?"* By Bryan M. Wolfe on Mon March 19th, 2012 Discusses privacy concerns expressed by users regarding this app.

http://appadvice.com/appnn/2012/03 /why-does-the-new-ipads-dictation- feature-require-a-wi-fi-connection

With the Dictation app you can write an email, send a text, search the web, or create a note. And you can do it all with only your voice. Instead of typing, tap the microphone icon on the keyboard and then say what you want to say while your iPad listens.

Like a voiceover app, this app is also a great tool to use for students with vision deficiencies.

Price: Free
(This app is built into version 3.)

### Evernote

A multi-platform cloud-sharing tool. It can take notes in multiple ways, save them to your cloud account, then share them or pull them down on almost any device. Everything in Evernote is searchable.

A student can use Evernote to complete research for a project and share that research with the teacher. They can add articles by adding the "clipper" tool to the app. They can also add their own thoughts and ideas as they read articles. When students take notes in class, they can use Evernote and share those notes with other students. Teachers can use Evernote in the same way, for researching and for taking and organizing their notes and being able to search for them all in one place.

Price: Free

Everything in Evernote is searchable, even this photograph of a whiteboard taken with the teacher's phone.

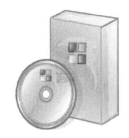

## Dragon Speak

Paraphrase Immediately using Dragon Speak

Another free strategy to enhance short-term memory so information isn't "gone" in two seconds is to have a student paraphrase what you just taught.

For example, after you've taught something important, ask a volunteer to paraphrase that information for the class. Most likely, your students will not relate the information in the same words you used, which will be novel to the brain.

This strategy only takes seconds to do, yet it lets your students hear the information again, in a different way, with a different voice. The brain likes novelty and, as a result of this strategy,  will remember the information better.

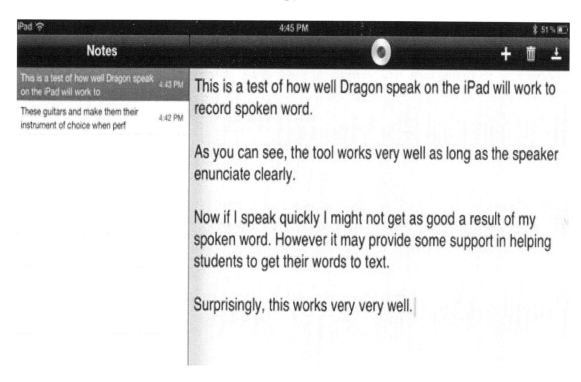

## Mendeley App

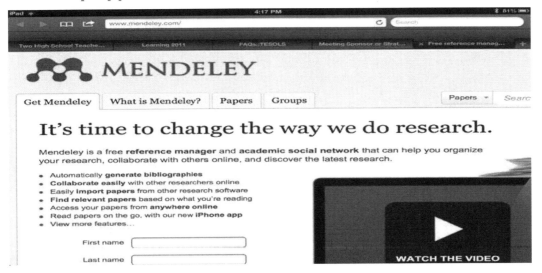

Mendeley is academic software that indexes and organizes all of your PDF documents and research papers into your own personal digital library. It gathers document details from your PDFs, allowing you to effortlessly search, organize, and cite. Basically, with Mendeley you are able to find all of your PDF files in one place.

Price: Free

### Droideley

Droideley is an unofficial Mendeley. Still in beta testing.

Price: Free

## *Bright Ideas*

## Chapter 6 – Visual Cues To Reach All Learners

Children today most often remember what they see better than what they hear, so appealing to a student's visual senses is something valuable to understand when teaching. After all, visual stimulation is paramount to teaching this visually-driven generation. Instead of rejecting it, we must step into their world and embrace it. Then, turn it around to stimulate learning.

# Provide Meaningful Visual Cues

✳ The brain thinks in pictures

Nonlinguistic representation

66

### The Brain Thinks in Pictures

When learning a subject for the first time, a student might grasp the information better if it's given to them in pictures first and not just words. For example, teach history by showing pictures of former presidents as they looked in their time instead of just telling students to read their biographies. Or, teaching new vocabulary words by using cartoons that act out the definitions of the words. The use of visual cues helps to "paint a picture" in the student's mind so that the memory becomes etched in their brain.

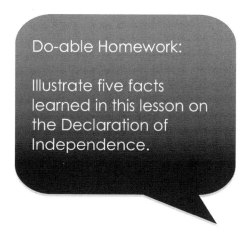

Do-able Homework:

Illustrate five facts learned in this lesson on the Declaration of Independence.

**Declaration of Independence**

The public act by which the Second Continental Congress, on July 4, 1776, declared the Colonies to be free and independent of England.

To declare          Your Freedom

Declaration of Independence

Sean McCready
High School Social Studies
Electronic Classrooms of Tomorrow, Ohio

## Teaching Vocabulary with Visuals

What if we taught English vocabulary in the same way we teach foreign languages? Popular language-learning programs teach vocabulary with visuals – meaningful pictures and other visual cues that the student can easily relate to. Similar strategies can be very effective in the classroom when students are learning words and concepts that are new to them.

Several flashcard packages are available to help teach vocabulary using visuals. *Vocabulary Cartoons*, from New Monic Books, links vocabulary words with memorable cartoons and captions in order to reinforce understanding and memorization (http://www.vocabularycartoons.com). Philip Geer's *Picture These SAT Words in a Flash*, from Barron's Educational Series (available on Amazon.com), uses a similar approach. These sources both have SAT and ACT vocabulary and *Vocabulary Cartoons* carries generic vocabulary programs for various grade levels.

I bought their flashcards, sorted through them, and actually found words I had never heard of. One of these was "antediluvian." I love the way it rolls off the tongue. But what does it mean? Antediluvian means prehistoric, ancient, and/or before the flood in the Bible.

The picture on the card is Auntie Lil who is eating dill pickles and reading a book titled _Before the Flood_. The flood was ancient, and so is Auntie Lil. Remember this: Auntie, a dill-lovin' lady, is eating pickles and reading a book about very old times. The pronunciation is "auntie-dill-luvian." You can see it in your head –

Auntie Dill (pickle) Lovin' Lady. If you flip the card over, you see the definition and some sample sentences using the word.

*Picture These SAT Words in a Flash* vocabulary cards are somewhat similar. They have a picture on one side and analogies on the other side, along with antonyms, synonyms, and sentences.

These catchy visual connections work for many students. You might ask, "But what if our SAT test words aren't on the cards? What if I can't afford to buy them?" Thankfully, these flashcard sets aren't the only way to learn vocabulary with a visual connection.

Rosetta Stone is a computer-based example of a program that successfully builds vocabulary skills combining visuals with auditory feedback and repetition.

## Vocabulary Apps

Vocabulary impacts test scores, reading comprehension, and fluency. The internet, and the App Store, contains a variety of vocabulary cartoon apps that can be used in the classroom to teach your students new words. The more interesting the cartoon, the more the student will remember the word and even learn to incorporate that word into everyday sentences. This may even encourage them to write stories of their own using their vocabulary words. (This would be a great time to introduce another type of app to teach writing – books and comics.)

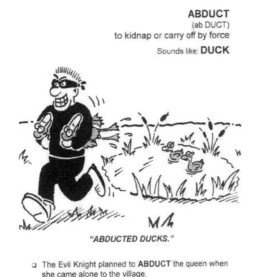

**ABDUCT**
(ab DUCT)
to kidnap or carry off by force
Sounds like: **DUCK**

"ABDUCTED DUCKS."

❑ The Evil Knight planned to **ABDUCT** the queen when she came alone to the village.

**CANNON**
A weapon the fires a big round black ball.

Sounds like: **"Shannon"**

A girl named **Shannon** blasted a **cannon**.

**MakeBeliefsComix.com**

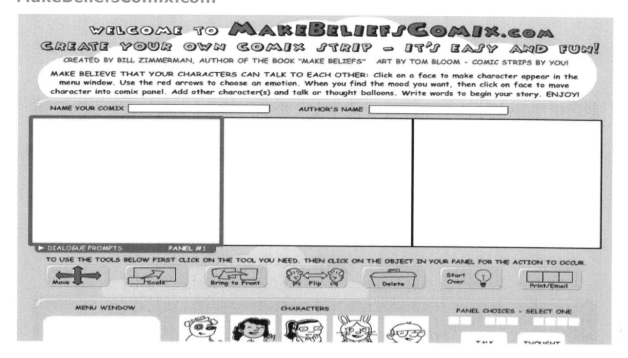

Make a vocabulary cartoon or comic strip
Form pictures to connect to vocabulary for visual vocabulary review cards.
Try http://www.makebeliefscomix.com, a site with wonderful tools for teachers and students alike. This can be used in or out of the classroom. Teachers can print them for students to take home as a homework assignment.
Price: Free

## Strip Designer

Photos can be added from the camera, your photo-album, or downloaded directly from your Facebook account. You can apply filters to photos and change the layout of the page to fit your needs. You can even paint on the photos or draw your own sketches from scratch.

Price: $2.99

Use comic strip makers and drawing apps to incorporate technology into research-based practice: Non-linguistic representation.

## Storyboards for Reading Comprehension

To make a storyboard, have students fold a piece of paper into squares and draw about what they read. They might do this while they read a story for the first time, as a review with a partner, or for homework after a reading assignment. The process of turning verbal information into a visual format reinforces the learning and helps keep the information in working memory longer.

I worked with a teacher who used this strategy with her middle school students. She asked them to draw a storyboard for homework and she gave permission to use the paint program on their computer at home if they wished – so they could either draw it by hand or use the paint program. She was shocked at what came back the next day because her students, whether they used the computer or not, put so much detail into their storyboards. She was clear that they got the information they needed from the reading. She said, "You know, I would never know how well they understood this information if I had assigned a worksheet."

Some students are not as visual as others, so these strategies offer a wonderful opportunity to use peer teaching. Have students pair up and explain their drawings to each other. They can correct or enhance their own drawing while discussing it with their partner.

## Create a Sequence Chart

When students need to remember the sequence of events in a story or historical events in order, making a sequence chart for homework is a good option. A sequence chart is like a timeline or storyline, and can be drawn on any type of paper, although long adding machine tape works well. Ask students to illustrate with drawings AND describe with words each event in chronological order. To remember information in sequence, such as a timeline in history, a cycle in science, or the chronology of a story, use adding machine tape or strips of paper and have students draw their storyboard in sequence. Now they can see the sequence of the storyline, timeline, or process literally in a visual, sequential format. This is a great way to reach kids who struggle with sequences because it reinforces the information with a research-based strategy: non-linguistic representation.

## Draw It So You Know It – Non-Linguistic Representation

Condense information into a picture and embrace the power of coloring. Teachers often present information verbally and linguistically. However, many of our students are visual learners. A substantial amount of our brainpower is devoted to visual processing. When teachers add a visual component, a drawing component, to what they are teaching, student recall increases. For example, after teaching for five or six minutes, or up to ten minutes in a high school class, give students three to five minutes to draw a picture, diagram, or symbol of what they just learned. This strategy allows students to take the verbal linguistic information just taught and turn it into visual information. This lets the brain process and use information in a different way which, in turn, helps students to better remember what has been taught.

When we use drawing exercises in the classroom, we often encounter resistance from students. They complain that they can't draw. One way to address this is to draw badly when we draw in the classroom. Use stick figure drawings and emphasize the importance of simple line drawings over drawing well. The point is to create an image that helps us remember what we've learned, not to get graded on our art.

If students say they can't draw, pair them up with someone who doesn't mind drawing. It would be a shame to lose students because of their initial resistance to doing something so different from what they are used to doing in school. The brain has a huge capacity for visual processing, so the visual component of our memory is very powerful.

## Tux Paint

This app is a computer art software for kids ages 3-12. It is used in schools around the world as a computer literacy drawing activity. It combines an easy-to-use interface, fun sound effects, and an encouraging cartoon mascot who guides children as they use the program. (Tux Paint Config, a separate program allows parents and teachers to change options – like turn off the sound. There are some accessibility controls.)
For elementary students this would be a fun and creative app to use in or out of the classroom.

Price: Free

## Picasso

Picasso

Draw, Paint, Doodle!

It's simple and intuitive to use, has an almost infinite pallette of colors, and has excellent brush effects.

Price: Free

## Drawing Pad

So far, this is the best app for capturing the printed text within pictures. It is a mobile art studio. Students can create their own art using "actual-sized" photo-realistic crayons, markers, paint brushes, colored pencils, stickers, roller pens and even more drawing supplies. This is not only useful for art classes, but also for academic classes when students are doing a creative project and they want to use original art to tell a story.

This app is useful for all grade levels to encourage creative fun.

The beautiful user interface puts the fun into creating art!

Price: $1.99

## Wet Paint

Get creative with Wet Paint 2.0.

This app is fun for adults and simple enough for kids to use.

Price: Free
(Pro version available)

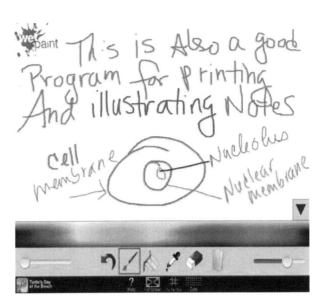

## Use "Meaningful" Color

Use color. Studies show that we remember color first and content second, so highlight or use colorful markers and pens to write vocabulary words and their definitions. Use different colors to make key words of the definition stand out and to help students remember the meaning of words.

Research shows that we learn better with color than with black and white text because color makes text unique, and the brain remembers what is unique. This is another reason to have students take their notes with colored fine tip markers or gel pens.

When students can accent their notes and their writing in different colors and make key words, letters, and other critical information stand out by writing it, bolding it, or underlining it in a different color, they will remember it better.

## Skitch

With Skitch, I can take a screen shot of anything on my iPad and pull it into Skitch and take notes on the screenshot.

I've heard of some teachers using Skitch in their classroom to show a journey on a map by taking a screenshot from Google Earth and uploading it, then creating a diagram for students to view.

Price: Free

## Pic Collage

Pic Collage is an extremely easy to use collage maker. It can be used for any study or homework assignment where a collage would be appropriate.

Price: Free

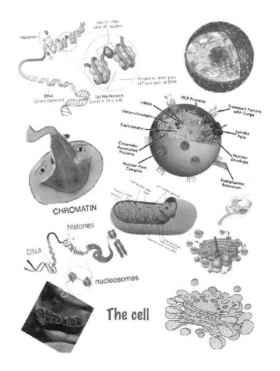

## Steps to Using Graphic Notes

Preview the chapter or section of your reading.
Choose an image that is central to the topic.
Choose 4 areas of emphasis (may be subtopics).
Jot down key ideas under each heading.

### RealWorld Paint

This app allows you, or your students, to create an image from scratch or edit one of your own images. It also has many special effects, similar to Photoshop, like image blending, shadow effects, and retouching tools.

Price: Free

## Cognitive Maps A.K.A. Mind Mapping[1]

Have students create a cognitive map with words and pictures to help them remember the sequence of events in a story or lesson. Using colored pencils and crayons, or even a computer, students can create a step-by-step map of the story, or process, complete with descriptions of events and drawings or clip art to help them remember what happened.

## Inspiration Software

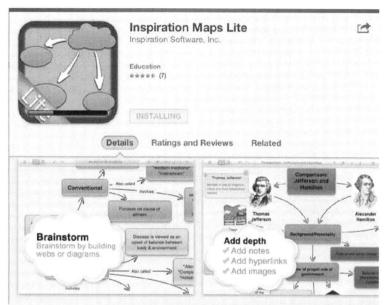

This is a website program that introduced an iPad app earlier this year. It promotes visual learning through the use of diagrams and cognitive mapping. It is a very useful tool to teach students the connection between different ideas or stories. This is a great tool to use in the classroom, especially for visually-driven students.

Price: Free*
*Free to try - five times. However, even in the first try, it continually hijacks the app to take you to the iPad store. It's extremely annoying. So, the price is *really* $9.99

---

[1] Developing cognitive maps and using advance organizers also increases critical thinking skills. (Barba and Merchant 1990; Snapp and Glover 1990; Tierney, et al. 1989).

## OmniGraffle

Need to create a quick diagram, process chart, page layout, website wireframe, or graphic design? With OmniGraffle, your iPad touch screen is your canvas (or graph paper, or whiteboard, or cocktail napkin...).

Price: $49.99

## XMind Portable App

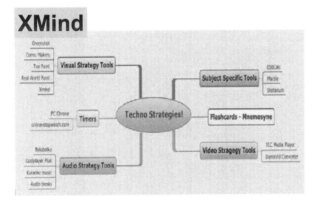

XMind is a cognitive mapping app that can be used in a classroom setting. It is used to draw diagrams to show relationships between different ideas. This is a great visual tool to help students understand how ideas or tasks connect. This can be used at all grade levels. Elementary: teaching comparison/contrast, story mapping, similarities/differences; Middle/High School: Essay brainstorming, story outlines, History timelines and outlines.

XMind has a very business-like look to it compared to other apps like it, and it is also customizable.

Price: Free
(Completely free - no trial version)

## Word Cloud

This is an extremely basic app; it uses white words on a black background. It is also a mind-mapping app for organizing thoughts and ideas. It creates pictures of "clouds" that act as floating collections of information. It is not as detailed and professional-looking, however, as other apps offering the same thing.

I felt that this app was not worth my time. Reviews of this app said that it was not a useful app at all, especially for the classroom.

Price: Free

## Thesaurus

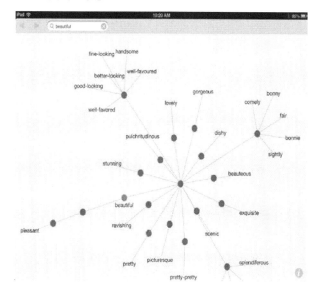

If you've ever been stuck trying to think of another word to describe something, you probably wished you had a thesaurus on hand to help you quickly find the word. This is what the Thesaurus app will do for you.

You will find the right synonym or antonym for just about every word. This is a great tool for both teachers and students to conveniently have with them.

Each search is quick and easy so you don't have to flip through pages in a book to find the word.

Price: $0.99

## Popplet for iPad

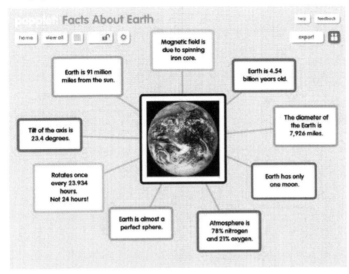

Popplet for iPad video review @ http://www.youtube.com/watch?v=sJMgm76qjfg

Have students create a cognitive map with words and pictures to help them remember the sequence of events in a story or history lesson. Using Popplet, you can use colored pencils and crayons, or even a computer, students can create a step-by-step map of the story complete with descriptions of events and drawings, or clip art to help them remember what happened.

Price: Free

## Smart Diagram Lite

Organize ideas and thoughts with clear diagrams. Simple & Easy.

Price: Free
Pro Price: $4.32

## Inkflow

Use Inkflow as if you're using a pen. Inkflow works like a word-processor for visual thinking. With it you can capture your ideas as easily as with pen and paper, then arrange and reorganize them with your fingers.

Price: Free
(Pro version available)

Inkflow allows you to draw something with your fingers and resize it. This app is good for teachers and students, especially students with learning disabilities like Down's Syndrome, who can better express themselves through art.

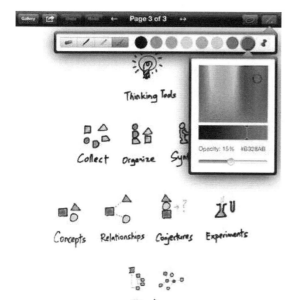

The pro version is significantly better than the free version allowing color and many other design options.

Must make an in-app purchase after the free download in order to get more pen colors to work with.

I chose not to pay for the app given the comparable features other free apps provide.

## *Bright Ideas*

# Chapter 7 – Old Techniques with Added Twists

There are always lessons to be learned from the past, especially when they turn out to be successful. Every teacher knows that the teachers that have gone before them and the techniques they used are oftentimes the best resources. However, in adapting to the times we live in and its technological influences, we must use the resources and lessons used in the past and put a bit of a spin on them. This is where iPad apps come in.

## Good Ole' Fashioned Flash Cards

There is tremendous value in repeating information while working with it to help move that information to long-term memory. One great way to accomplish this is through good old-fashioned drill and practice. When asking students to remember certain kinds of information, drill and practice activities are critical to getting that information through working memory and into long-term memory. One of my favorite drill and practice activities is an updated approach to the tried and true flash card. For instance, when teaching phonics rules at the elementary level, have your students print their words on flash cards rather than writing them three times each. The brain remembers print because it makes a clear visual picture. When they print their words, have them put the phonics rules they're learning that week in a different color so it stands out.

If students are having trouble with certain parts of a spelling or a vocabulary word, have them use a contrasting color for the part of the word they are struggling with.

All students, especially those who consistently fail the spelling sections of vocabulary tests, or spelling tests in the lower grades, will benefit from these strategies. Have them review their cards, by themselves or with a partner, at least once or twice every day.

I have watched students who consistently fail the spelling sections of vocabulary tests or spelling tests in the lower grades use picture-enhanced flash card drill and practice strategies. As long as they review their cards, either by themselves or with a partner, once or twice a day and remove the cards they know well, their grades go up.

Have students make their own flashcards by looking up vocabulary words online and finding pictures that show the definitions. Ask students to print the picture, glue it on a card, then write a silly sentence under the picture to help them remember the word, and write the definition on the back. If your students don't have internet access, have them get creative and draw the pictures themselves!

## Flashcards+ App

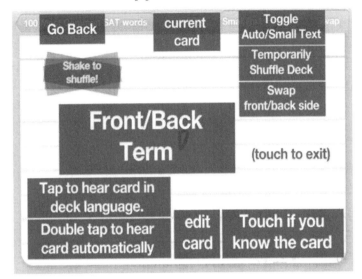

This is a really good and useful app for students. Many students learn and process information better when they can narrow it down to an index card. When they don't have to read through a whole chapter, but can put the chapter information into flashcard format to study, wherever they go, all on one mobile device app. This is certainly an app I would recommend for middle and high school students.

You can also access tens of millions of pre-made decks for free.

Price: Free

There are countless flash card programs available for the iPad or iPhone. Almost all of them are subject specific, thereby making it difficult to assess the validity or quality of any one of them. My suggestion is to find a flash card app for these topic that you are trying to study and thoroughly explore the free version. Also, try to find reviews of the flash card app online.

## Quizlet for iPad

A great way for students to study directly from the mobile device. Pick from three mobile-only study modes to suit your learning style and take advantage of audio in 18 languages to reinforce pronunciation and retention. Plus, with full offline support you can study anywhere — even without an internet connection.

Price: Free

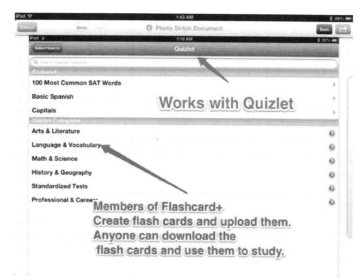

This app may not be effective for every subject, however, it certainly supports a wide variety of memorization tasks.

## Flashcards Buddy Pro

This flash card app is rated highest in the Google Play store and supports a variety of flash card functions.

Price: $1.99
(Try the free demo version first)

## Mnemmosyne

this is a portable app that lives on a flash drive and works with your PC. It is a basic flash card program.

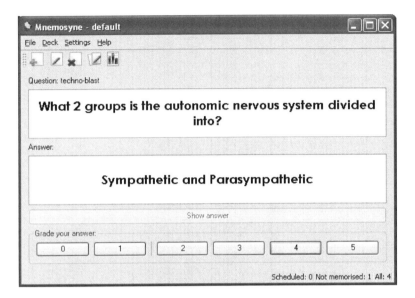

## FlashcardExchange.com

Flashcardexchange.com is an excellent web based or browser-based flash card studying system. It is not as fancy as some others that are available. However, I like that other users might import flash cards that my students can use for their studying purposes.

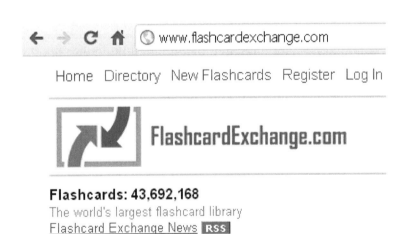

## *Bright Ideas*

# Chapter 8 – The Power of Music

Rewrite karaoke songs with information students need to learn
Link old tunes with concepts: replace the words of a familiar song with information students must memorize.
Put the words to music!

Ever notice how you can easily remember the words to *The Itsy Bitsy Spider* and other songs you may not have sung since childhood? That's because the rhythm and rhyme of music helps you to remember the lyrics. This idea can be used to help students memorize vocabulary words by turning the words' definitions into song lyrics or by writing lyrics using sentences that put the words into an easy to understand context. (ELL: Rewrite a song by changing the verb tense or substituting nouns and adjectives.)

## Use Music

The deep part of our brain, the part that's more primitive, remembers music. Music is a powerful learning tool that is being used all over the country to increase long-term memory and boost state test scores.

One teacher taught the rules for long division using the tune and movement of the *Macarena*. When it came time for the math section of the state test, the test proctor knew exactly which kids were in this teacher's class because every now and then, one of them would stand up and start doing the *Macarena*. Then they would sit back down and begin to write.

Some kids won't sing 'silly' songs like algebraic equations to *God Bless America* or the quadratic formula to the tune of the Notre Dame Fight Song. In these cases, teachers use karaoke CDs or MP3s with current popular music and have their students rewrite the lyrics to fit the needs of the course material. Music is a powerful strategy. You can take anything you want students to learn, find any kind of rhyme or music they already know, and have them substitute the lyrics with material you are trying to teach.

## CoolPlayer

This app is an MP3 player with Freeform skin support. It features a playlist editor.

Price: Free

This app is downloadable for Apple and Android users. It can also be downloaded to your hard drive to play on your computer

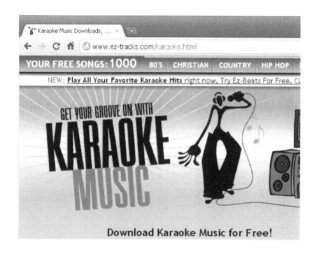

## Karaoke Music

With the right equipment you can utilize music and put the talents of your students on display. It also makes for a fun day in music class. Or you can even use it with a project in History or English class.

Price: Free

## Garage Band

I had not seen the academic value of GarageBand with the exception of using it in a music class or program until I saw how a teacher had her students create their own background music for project videos instead of using ready-made music they might find online. This avoided any copyright infringement, as well as challenged students to use it. Their imagination and skill to create unique background music.

This also had the advantage of giving the musically inclined to students a way to contribute to a content subject area project.

Students would have to use their analytical skills, or trial and error, or research skills to figure out how to use GarageBand to create the music. There is academic benefit in that exercise.

## *Bright Ideas*

# Chapter 9 – Teaching with Video Clips

Interweave your lesson with video clips that provide meaning and background for the topic being taught. Limit clips to 3-6 minutes.

## Apps that capture and play video:

### Damn Vid

A video downloader. While DamnVid can convert local video files, it can also download video streams from most video sharing websites. But what gives it the edge over other video downloaders and converters is that not only does it do both the downloading and the converting, but it does them at the same time; it converts as it downloads, making the whole process much faster.
DamnVid has a built-in YouTube video search. Search and download directly from within the app!

Price: Free

## VLC Player

This is one of the more popular media players on any platform. Take your audio and video files along with everything you need to play them on the go. You can place it on your USB flash drive, iPod, portable hard drive or a CD and use it on any computer or iPad.

Price: Free

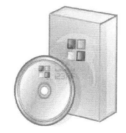

## Brain Pop Movie

This is a very popular education and numerously downloaded app because it brings learning to your fingertips. Watch a different animated movie every day, then test your new knowledge with an interactive quiz – free!

Price: Free

Interesting review of iTunes University:
http://www.danpontefract.com/my-thoughts-ibooks-2-itunes-u-app-ibooks-author/

## iTunes University - for Video

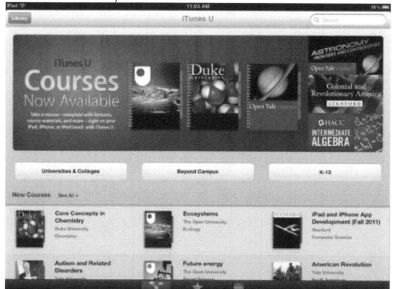

"From the iTunes U app, students can play video or audio lectures and take notes that are synchronized with the lecture. They can read books and view presentations. See a list of all the assignments for the course and check them off as they're completed. And when you send a message or create a new assignment, students receive a push notification with the new information."

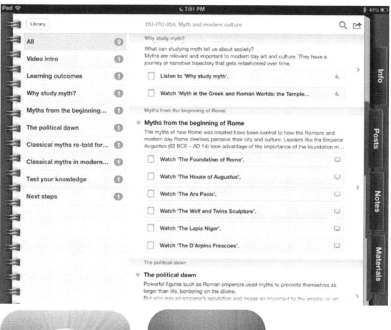

## *Bright Ideas*

# Chapter 10 – English/Language Arts Apps

## Reading

Reading has always been fundamental to learning. Readers do not become readers unless it is taught and modeled to them. So, read to youth often. It will:

Expose them to higher levels of vocabulary
Model the importance of looking up and defining unknown words
Raises their instructional level and above

According to the <u>National Center for Education Statistics (NCES)</u>, a division of the U.S. Department of Education, children who are read to at home enjoy a substantial advantage over children who are not:
26% of children who were read to three or four times in the last week by a family member recognized all letters of the alphabet. This is compared to 14 percent of children who were read to less frequently.
The NCES also reported that children who were read to frequently are also more likely to:
count to 20, or higher than those who were not (60% vs. 44%)
write their own names (54% vs. 40%)
read or pretend to read (77% vs. 57%)
According to NCES, only 53 percent of children ages three to five were read to daily by a family member (1999). Children in families with incomes below the poverty line are less likely to be read to aloud everyday than are children in families with incomes at or above poverty.
The more types of reading materials there are in the home, the higher students are in reading proficiency.

## Audio Books

Listen to Audio Books as an alternative to T.V., DVD, and video games
Audio books combine important ingredients in creating a successful lifelong reader. Audio books:

- Motivate students to read.
- Allow students to enjoy a book at their interest level that might be above their reading level.
- Allow slower readers to participate in class activities
- Provide a way to learn the patterns of language, learn expressions, and increase vocabulary.
- Are good examples of fluent reading for children, young adults and for people learning English as a second language.
- Build the neural connections necessary for auditory processing skills. Auditory processing skills are required for literacy.
- Improve listening skills.
- For pre-reading, it familiarizes students with the story so that students can concentrate on the words when they read the text.
- Bring a book to life, thereby inspiring, entertaining, and linking language and listening to the reading experience.
- Build a reading scaffold--broadening vocabularies, stretching attention spans, flexing thinking skills.

Recorded Book Rentals: http://www.recordedbooks.com
Books on Tape: http://www.booksontape.com
Chivers Audio Books:  http://www.theaudiobookstore.com/authors/c-j-chivers
 or (800) 621-0182
Blackstone Audiobooks: http://www.downpour.com/
The Teaching Company: http://www.thegreatcourses.com/
Sells taped lectures on history, literature, etc. Ask to hear their Free sample lecture on "How to Understand and Listen to Great Music," one of a series of 16 lectures on music.

Recording for the Blind & Dyslexic: http://www.learningally.org/
They have 75,000 unabridged books on tape. They also sell portable four-track cassette players ($99 - $199). Students can get textbooks custom-recorded; ask for information. Fees are $50.00 to apply and $25.00 per year thereafter for all the books you can read; no postage required. Application form includes a form for your doctor to sign, where applicable.

## Balabolka

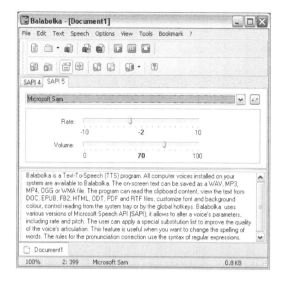

A text-to-speech (TTS) application that uses the built-in voices of MS Windows to read text on screen or any text passage you insert into the program. This is a great tool to support struggling readers, auditory learners, and English language learners.

Price: Free

## LibriVox

LibriVox Audio Books provides free access to over 6,000 audio books. Each audiobook can be streamed over the internet or downloaded for later use.

Price: Free

**Learn out Loud**

"Apple iTunes now features a section of their store called iTunes U, which features free audio & video downloads from dozens of universities across the United States and around the world including Stanford, Duke, MIT, Arizona State, and more.

At LearnOutLoud.com we combed through these free resources to pick out the best lectures, courses, and audio & video programs that iTunes U offers."

These websites offer access to a variety of royalty free and public domain books and publications. Use these resources as another way to support those struggling readers, auditory learners, and English Language Learners.

- *Audio Owl (http://www.booksshouldbeFree.com/)*
- *Thought Audio (http://www.thoughtaudio.com/)*

## iTunes University - for Audio Books

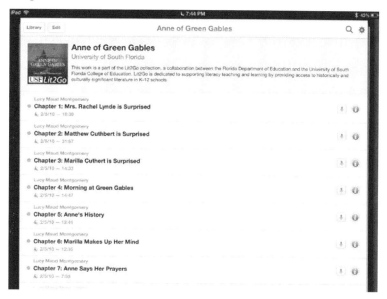

You can download a huge selection of audio books with iTunes University onto an iPad.

If there are choices when planning lessons with common core, check to see which common core book selections are available on iTunes University before planning your lessons.

## Free Books for iPad

23,469 classic books, with the ability to highlight, create notes, bookmarks and have dictionary support.

To get the audio book functionality, you need to upgrade to the pro version:

Price: Basic - no audio - Free
Pro Price: $3.99

## Amazon Kindle

Access your Kindle even if you don't have your Kindle with you by downloading it onto your iPad. This app automatically synchronizes your last page read between devices with Amazon Whispersync.

Adjust the text size, add bookmarks, and view the annotations you created on your Kindle. Get the best reading experience available.

Price: Free (the app is free and the only thing you would have to purchase would be any books purchased in the Amazon store.)

Any PDF document can be emailed to (your name)@kindle.com or (device name)@Kindle.com and the PDF can be pulled into Amazon to read it.

That said, I would use PDF Notes to read any document that I may want to notate, write on, etc. Amazon's iPad kindle reader does not have any note taking options.

  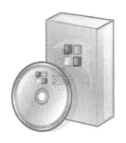 

## Barnes & Nobel NOOK

## 24/7 Tutor - Learn languages

"24/7 Tutor goes beyond the simple talking phrasebook or flashcard program, providing a set of engaging, interactive study tools that help you really learn the language."

Price: Free

## Google Translate App

Functional app for English language learners as well as students taking a foreign language.

Can also be used as a method of translate and correct practice because often Google Translate does not translate correctly.

While in France, I used it to ask how to turn on the heat in my room. What I really asked was, "How do I set a fire in my room?"

Price: Free

## Toontastic for iPad

Toontastic is a storytelling and creative learning tool that enables kids to draw, animate, and share their own cartoons with friends and family around the world through simple and fun imaginative play! It's like putting together your own puppet show. The recommended ages for this app is 4-7 and 8-10

Price: Free

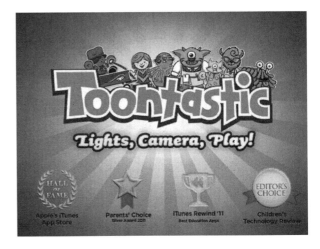

The number of characters and settings keeps expanding with the addition of themed scene packs – but these packs must be purchased for an additional $.99 each.

## Puppet Pals HD

A simple-looking app with a tremendous amount of potential for secondary application in all subject areas.

Price: Free

## Dictionary.com

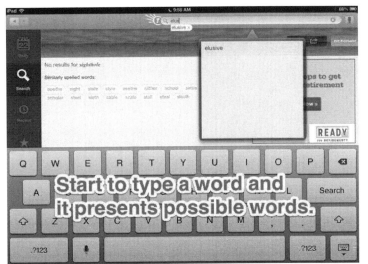

The trusted online dictionary in app form!

Provides definitions and synonyms (thesaurus). Also works offline.

Price: Free with ads and limitations

Upgrade price: $4.99 - no ads and examples of the words used in sentences,

## Dictionary.com Flashcards

The flash card version is originally an iPhone app so it does not present in horizontal mode

Price: Free

## Vocabology

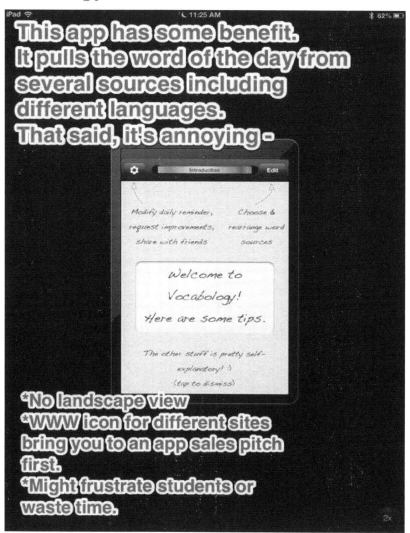

The makers have an interesting approach to upgrade. Rather than pay a fee to upgrade, you must purchase one of the other products that show up on their bookshelf.

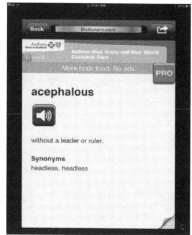

## Mad Libs

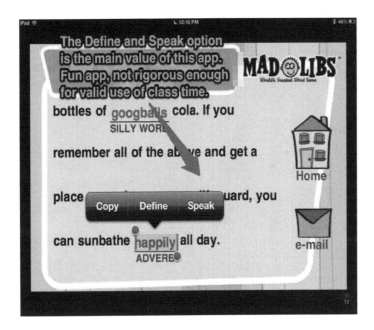

How To Enjoy Yourself on the Beach is Free.

Other Mad Libs stories in the app: Price: $3.99*

*Save your money. Spend it on the real Mad Lib pads that we all grew up with. That's a better investment.

Android has a variety of similar apps available. Just search for Mad Libs in Google Play to find equivalent apps.

## Sentence Builder TEEN by Mobile Education

I purchased this app after reading a very positive review of the app from someone who praised the app developer for considering quality apps for teens.

The main problem with this app is that it is too easy for students to simply guess which of the two or three choices is correct.

I'm sure there are appropriate uses for this app, however, unless a teacher is sitting with the student, I doubt there is much value in the process for most teens.

Price: $5.99

## Grammar Up HD

By Eknath Kadam

Grammar Up is an interactive app that can help learners to improve their grammar, word selection, and vocabulary.   Custom timer settings can assist learners to improve response times under exam time constraints. Students are able to study all of the grammar rules by topic.

Price: Free

This app is dry, boring, and no different than using a worksheet on an iPad.

By Kuber Tech
**Beware**: There are two Grammar Up apps. The version by Kuber Tech has higher user ratings than the version by Eknath Kadam

NOTE: The Grammar UP above and the Grammar UP in this row are different applications!

Price: $4.99

Android Version by ElmatjLada

Price: $2.99

NOTE: Check out Grammar Guru

## Shakespeare in Bits

A new, exciting, multimedia approach to learning and teaching Shakespeare's plays. Shakespeare In Bits brings The Bard's most popular plays to life through magnificently animated re-enactment, full audio and unabridged text in one comprehensive package.

As the video rolls, the text that aligns with the video highlights in red.

Price: Free for demo version. You get a sample of the famous balcony scene of Romeo & Juliet.

Most of the plays, each sold separately, sell for either $9.99 or 14.99

My Play Library

Currently Viewing:

Launch

Julius Caesar

In the last days of the Roman Republic, a conspiracy, born of both virtue and jealousy, is hatched to bring down the greatest roman of all time.

JULIUS CAESAR JUST LAUNCHED

News

## English Idioms Illustrated

This is an absolutely gorgeous app. I learned so much about the origin of idioms from it. The free version gives you a good amount to work with.

## Idioms Lite

Not even close to as appealing as *English Idioms Illustrated*

**Bright Ideas**

# Chapter 11 – Mathematics Apps

## Model and Solve Equations Using Manipulatives

Using manipulatives is the only way some students can truly understand the concepts being taught. Unfortunately, a prevailing myth in secondary education, especially high schools, is that manipulatives are for elementary children only. I am a strong advocate for using manipulatives and concrete representation for teaching math to students at the secondary level, including high school students.

## Research Background

Using manipulatives provides students a meaningful context for mathematical knowledge and helps them understand fundamental relationships associated with the knowledge (B. S. R. Witzel, Richard W.; Riccomini, Paul J. ; Moore , Eugene T. , 2010). Multiple embodiments – the use of many different models – allow students to focus on common characteristics and generalize to the abstract. "Helping students make connections between the concrete (e.g., models and manipulatives) and the abstract (e.g. generalizations and symbolic representations) facilitates understanding, promotes success at learning, and helps relieve mathematics anxiety" (Reys, 2009, p. 17).

In regards to secondary math, such as Algebra, Henri Picciotto[2] (Henri Picciotto, 2010) writes:
*Even though they cannot make algebra easy, manipulatives can play an important role in the transition to a new algebra course. They provide access to symbol manipulation for students who had previously been frozen out of the course because of their weak number sense. They provide a geometric interpretation of symbol manipulation, thereby enriching all students' understanding, and making a powerful connection to another part of mathematics. They support cooperative learning, and help improve discourse in the algebra class by giving students objects to think with and talk about. It is in the context of such reflection and conversation that learning happens.*

*There are four main commercial versions of algebra manipulatives. In order of their appearance on the market, they are Algebra Tiles (Cuisenaire), the Lab Gear (Creative Publications), Algeblocks (Southwestern Publishing), and Algebra Models (Classroom Products). All four provide a worthwhile model of the distributive law. However, note that only the Lab Gear and Algeblocks allow work in three dimensions.*

---

[2] From Henry Piccciotti's Web site (http://www.mathedpage.org)

Bradley Witzel is also an advocate of using manipulatives to teach math through algebra. He describes the Concrete Representation Abstract method (A. Witzel, 2007).(A. Witzel, 2007). The CRA sequence of instruction consists of teaching students to solve mathematics problems through three levels of instruction, from the manipulation of concrete objects to learning through pictorial representations to finally solving equations through abstract notation.(A. Witzel, 2007)

The CRA approach to teaching mathematics has proven to be beneficial to secondary students with math difficulties, from small group settings to whole-class instruction (B. S. Witzel, 2005). In fact, after receiving CRA instruction, students with learning disabilities had a success rate two to three times higher than their traditionally taught peers. According to Bradley S. Witzel, co-author of the book *Solving Equations- An Algebra Intervention* (B. S. R. Witzel, Richard W.;Riccomini,Paul J. ;Moore ,Eugene T. , 2010), CRA benefits students with math difficulties because it presents information in a multisensory way: visually, auditorily, tactilely, and kinesthetically. This multisensory approach causes the brain to process the information several times in various formats, making it easier for students to memorize, encode, and retrieve the information later. In addition, CRA helps students solve abstract problems without thinking fluently at the abstract level by giving them other levels of learning, whether pictorial or concrete, to turn to solve the problem (B. S. R. Witzel, Richard W.;Riccomini,Paul J. ;Moore ,Eugene T. , 2010).

## Technology and Math

## National Library of Virtual Manipulatives

## GeoGebra.org

This is a free and multi-platform dynamic mathematics software for all levels of education that joins geometry, algebra, tables, graphing, statistics and calculus in one easy-to-use package. Accessible for all computers and mobile devices.

Price: Free (must register and become a member in order to get all of the benefits.)

There is a video tutorial that lays out the inner workings of the site and how to use it.

Create graphs and charts and share them with other members of the site.

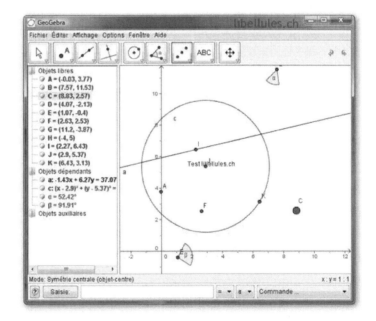

## Scientific Graphing Calculator

## Geoboard

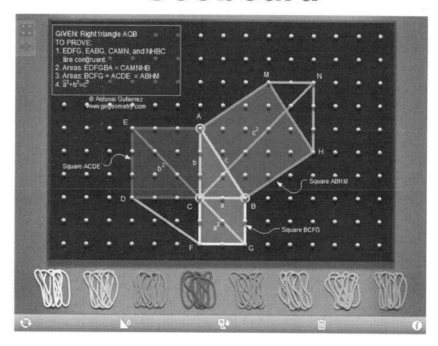

Apple has provided more interactive ways to make learning math engaging and fun for all students. Model and solve equations using manipulatives and visuals.

## Virtual Manipulatives - Fractions, Decimals, Percents

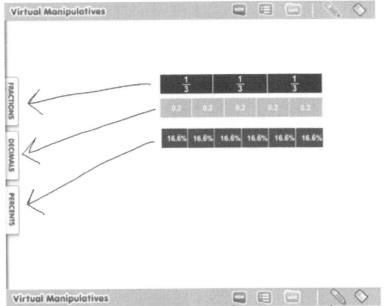

Virtual manipulatives supports student understanding of these critical concepts - concepts taught in elementary school and often still not mastered in high school.

Students can "physically manipulate" virtual manipulatives.

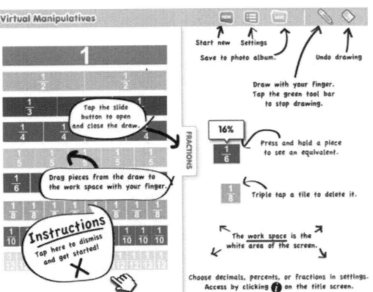

The app allows students to see equivalents to a solution that, at the secondary level ,is often presented solely in abstrat format.

Price: Free

## Equater iPhone App

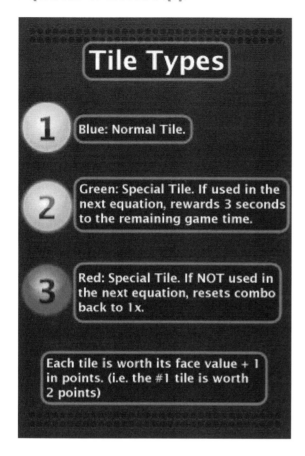

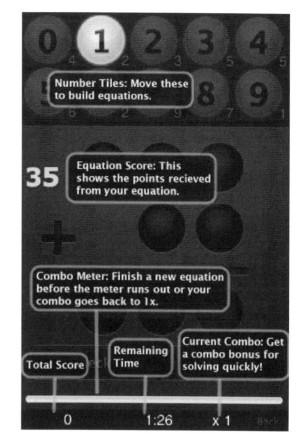

Equater is a race the clock math practice game. It appears to be elementary in value, however, it challenges the bran to think quickly, strategize, and focus to win.

Price: Free

For students who struggle to finish a timed math test on time, this app will support faster problem solving on the test because math facts become automatized

It's also a great brain exerciser for adults.

## Free GraCalc

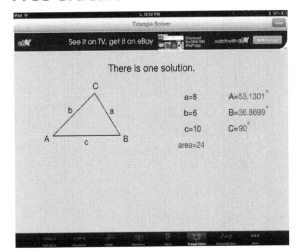

Purpose-built graphing calculators can easily cost upwards of a hundred dollars, but with this app you can have all of the power of a graphing calculator conveniently located on your Apple device, for free! There are also paid graphing calculator apps available.

Price: Free

### Algeo graphing calculator

*Marton Veges*
Draw functions, find intersections, and show a table of values of the functions with an easy to use interface.

Most popular graphing calculator in the Google Play store. Algeo is a graphing calculator with the best graphing capabilities.

Price: Free

## Multiplication of Fractions Using Manipulatives [3]

Geoboards are manipulative devices used to illustrate math operations such as fractions and geometry. Originally, they were made of wood with nails driven half way in and used with elastic bands to form shapes with the nails. Today, they are available in a variety of designs and materials, including online virtual geoboards, but the basic design of pegs on a board remains. In a math lesson plan provided in my book, *RTI Strategies for Secondary Teachers,* I use a geoboard to provide hands-on, visual representations of fractions.

Engineering professors at Rochester Institute of Technology, Worcester Polytechnic Institute, and Clarkson University have expressed to me their concern over the fact that many of the students in their engineering programs can plug in formulas to solve a math problem on paper, yet these same students cannot apply that math knowledge to building a physical product.

Additionally, college level technical programs all over the country understand, and embrace, the importance of hands-on practice and the use of manipulatives in their courses. Students at all ability levels need to not only understand abstract mathematical concepts, but also the concrete application of those concepts.

## Geoboard

Price: Free

Create line segments and polygons by stretching bands around the pegs. Choose from eight different band colors Fill individual shapes with a transparent color, or use the Fill All button to toggle all the bands between filled and unfilled. On the iPad, switch between the standard 25-peg board and the expanded board with 150 pegs. .

---

[33] Excerpted from "RTI Strategies for Secondary Teachers by Susan Gingras Fitzell, Corwin 2011

## iMathSg Lite

Some Topics covered :
1. Quadratic Equations on Word Problems.
2. Pythagoras' Theorem
3. Linear Graphs
4. Quadratic Graphs
5. Simultaneous Linear Equations
6. Simultaneous Equations on Word Problems

Excerpted from the iTunes store description because I can't say it any better:

"Published by The Sunday Times, Singapore , 17-October-2010 under Home section page 16.

*** EXTRACT OF THE ARTICLE *** Mathematics teacher Loh Cheng Yee may be pushing 60, but that has not stopped her from tuning in to the high-tech appetite of teenagers.

Late last month, the former Chinese High School and Catholic High School teacher launched two applications on the iTunes App Store to help secondary school students revise math on their iPhone or iPod Touch.

She is the first to put math workbooks based on the local school syllabus on such a platform.

'This is the best way to introduce new materials to students,' said Ms Loch, who has been teaching math in Singapore schools for three decades

Price: Lite version Free (Lite version is limited to two exercises per topic)

iMathSg Secondary Remix $0.99

## Mensuration

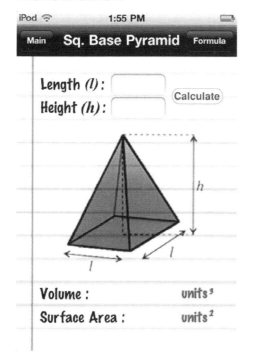

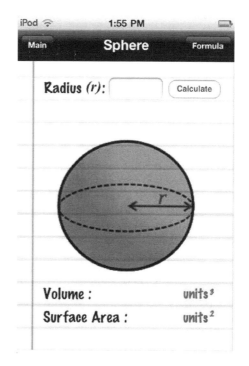

 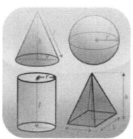

Merit award winner in i.code 2011 competition held by Nanyang Polytechnic (NYP) and Infocomm Development Authority of Singapore (IDA)

An app created by pupils for pupils.

This app calculates area and volume of solid objects such as spheres, cones, square pyramids and cylinders.

Price: Free

## Algebra Explained C.1 - Order of Operations LITE

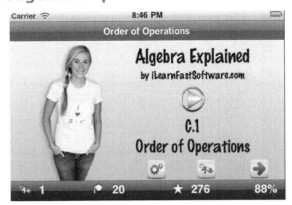

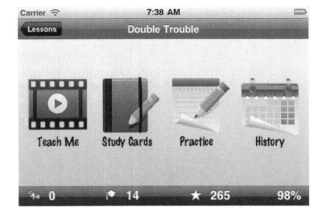

There is a series of apps that explain various topics in Algebra. Reviews say that it makes practice fun. Adults have used it to refresh their math.

Lite Price: Free

Full Version Price: $0.99

## DerivativeQ by PropedeutiQ.net

DerivativeQ helps you to find the symbolic derivative of functions.

Price: Free

## ESBCalc

ESBCalc (Math) is a Scientific Calculator that supports Infix Notation, Brackets, Scientific Functions (Trigonometric, Hyperbolic, Logarithmic "Base 10, Base 2 & Natural"), Memory, Paper Trail, Result History List and more. This is a great tool for showing students the process of mathematical problems, reinforcing visual learning, and teaching calculator skills.

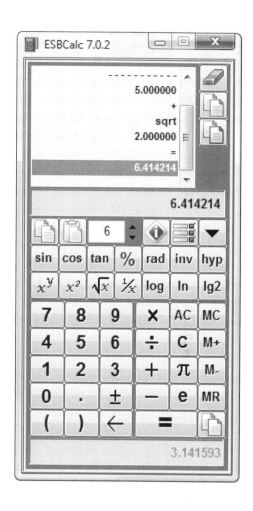

## Math Doodles

I've included Math Doodles to this book simply because of its beauty. Not only is there value in the practice of basic math skills, it's a work of art every time. If this app could excite a student to practice, then it is well worth the space on the iPad.

Price: Free

## *Bright Ideas*

# Chapter 12 – Science Apps

Students will use the iPad science apps to learn more about biology, physics, chemistry, anatomy, and much more. Apps like:

## 3DBrain

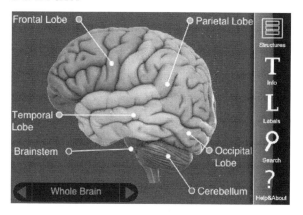
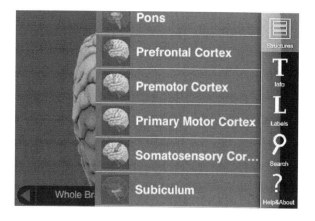

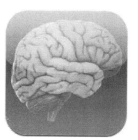

Rotate and zoom around 29 interactive structures. Discover how each brain region functions, what happens when it is injured, and how it is involved in mental illness. Each detailed structure comes with information on functions, disorders, brain damage, case studies, and links to modern research

Price: Free

## StarWalk

This app is so accurate that it's been called "unbelievable." StarWalk is a reality app that labels all the stars, constellations, and satellites you point your iPhone or iPad to. You can find out what constellation you've been looking at from your bedroom window and get a lot of exciting and educative information.

Price: $4.99

## Particle Zoo

Would you like to get to know the particles that make up our universe a little better? Then carry this convenient list of subatomic particles in your pocket! Based on The Particle Zoo plushies.

Price: Free

## K12 Periodic Table of the Elements by K12 Inc.

  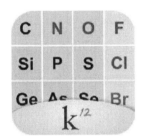

K12 Periodic Table of the Elements lets you explore the elements and their key attributes in a simple, easy-to-use way. It's a perfect reference for working through homework problems for Science courses.

Price: Free

## PopSci.com

PopSci.com delivers cutting edge scientific research, gadgets, and green tech. PopSci.com's news-reader apps deliver all the content from PopSci.com in an easy-to-read format.

Honestly, when I first clicked on the app I was stunned with how amazing it looked.

Price: Free

## Neutrons4Science

Enter the world of neutrons! This powerful and highly acclaimed tool is not only for the study of condensed matter (the world we live in) but also for confirming our current understanding of physics.

Price: $2.99

## VideoScience

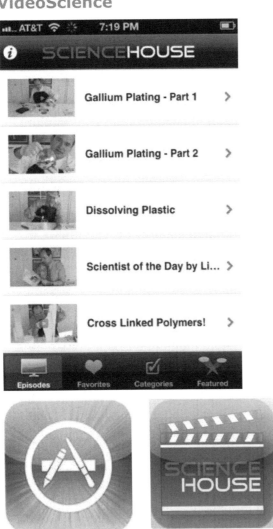

A growing library of over 80 hands-on Science lessons for both the home and the classroom. These short videos demonstrate inexpensive and easy-to-recreate experiments that are designed to inspire and excite kids of all ages.

Price: Free

**Bright Ideas**

# Chapter 13 – Social Studies Apps

Use history and geography apps to explore the world from past to present. Some of these apps may include:

### History: Maps of the World

This app is a fun and educational collection of high-resolution historical maps.

A great resource that offers students and teachers information about different countries and states during different periods of history.

You can click on any country and get a list of information about it, which makes it very interactive. There are also a large number of maps available, especially for an app that is free.

There is a catch to this app being free; there are many ads that stream across the screen when you have the app open, and, for some, this will be very distracting.

Price: Free (Pro version available)

## Virtual History ROMA

This app takes students on a fantastic voyage to Ancient Rome, the capital of the largest empire in the ancient world, which has been reconstructed in virtual form.

This app is very useful and informative for middle and high school students. It provides in-depth panoramic views of Ancient Rome, views you can't get from a textbook.

Price: $9.99

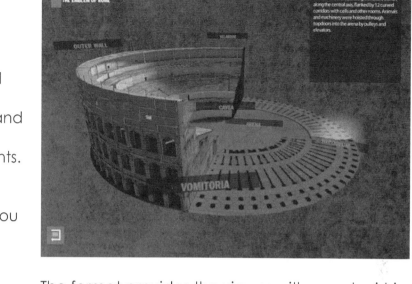

The format provides the viewer with an astonishing insight into Roman civilization, using innovative functions and multimedia content.

## AP U.S. History

This app covers everything from the European discovery of the New World to the present. Use this app to study with five pre-made flashcard decks, as the app is divided into a five section US History course.

Price: $2.99

## Geomaster Plus US

A true geography quiz to test your knowledge and to quickly become unbeatable. Find all of the states and place them on the map as fast as possible

Price: Free

## *Bright Ideas*

# Chapter 14 – Topics Across the Board

## Khan Academy by Khan Academy

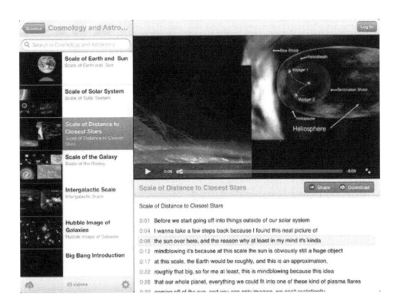

3,200 videos on everything from arithmetic to physics, finance, and history and hundreds of skills to practice. They are a not-for-profit with the goal of changing education for the better by providing a free world-class education for anyone anywhere.

Price: Free

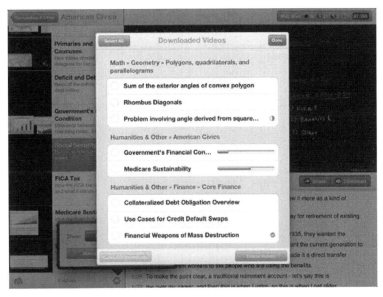

**KHAN**
ACADEMY

Several unofficial apps available

## Wolfram Alpha

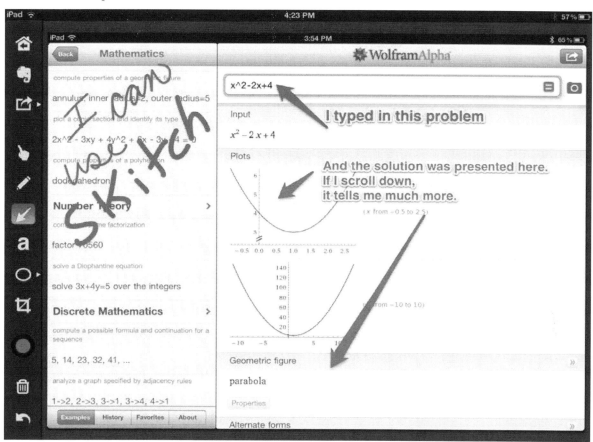

**Some topics covered:**
- Mathematics
- Physics
- Chemistry
- Earth Sciences
- Weather
- Geography
- People and History

A quote from my 22 year old son, who is in Engineering School, "Best math app ever! May have to pay to do the more complex fun stuff, but it's awesome and you can always go online and use it there too if you don't want to use the app."

## How Stuff Works

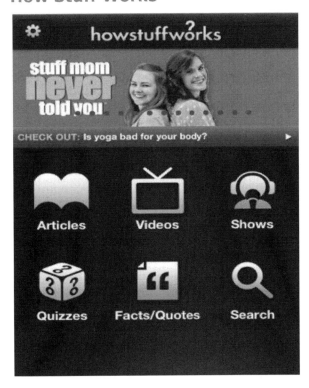

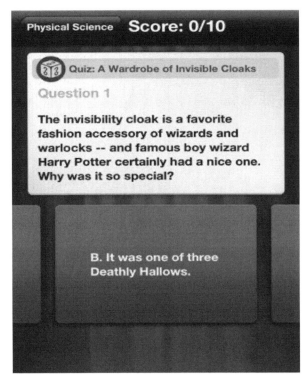

40,000+ articles! 12,000+ videos! 2,000+ shows! 1,000+ quizzes! Tweet your favorite podcasters while listening to their shows. Browse articles and the latest blog posts while you listen. Want to be the first to get the latest HSW info? Set up a push notification and you'll instantly be the first in the know!

30,000+ HowStuffWorks articles. Watch archived videos from both HowStuffWorks and the Discovery Channel!

Price: Free

## SAT Question of the Day for iPad

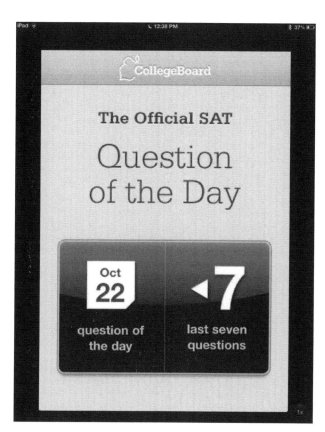

From sat.collegeboard.org, this website and app give users a chance to tease their brain with real SAT questions and SAT preparation materials from the test maker.

While there are books and other study materials available for a fee, the Question of the Day app is free.

Price: Free

SAT Word A Day AUDIO

Get a new SAT vocabulary word on your device every day.

There are several SAT prep apps available in Google Play

Price: Free

## *Bright Ideas*

# Chapter 15 – Apps Just for Teachers

There are a variety of apps that are created just for teachers that help to make our jobs more efficient when incorporating iPads into our instruction

**Dropbox**

Dropbox's lifesaving app is well worth mentioning. It allows you to upload your files to their site, access them from anywhere, and share with co-workers. An excellent choice just for the backup alone, but there are many other uses.

Price: Free

## Memeo Connect Reader

Connects with Google Docs. It has a VERY cool interface.

With most common document formats supported, you can read and view all your documents on-the-go, with the ease and speed of your iPhone or iPad. You will be able to read it without any WiFi or Internet connection.

Price: $4.99

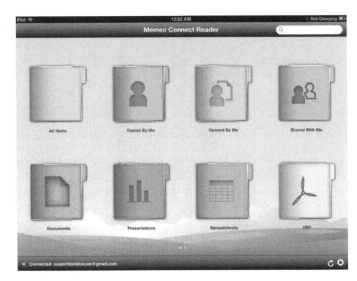

## Splashtop

PLAY THEN ANNOTATE OVER FLASH MEDIA

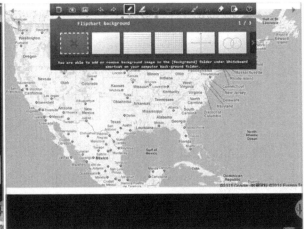

Turn your iPad into an interactive whiteboard. Connect to your computer over Wifi, then can watch Flash media with fully synchronized video and audio, control with PC and Mac applications, and annotate lesson content all from your iPad.

Price: 19.99

## Edmodo

This app makes it easy for teachers and students to stay connected and share information in one localized space. Use your iOS device to send notes, submit assignments, post replies, and check messages and upcoming events while away from the classroom.

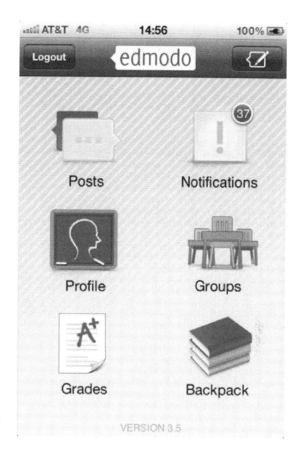

Teachers can post last-minute alerts to their students, keep tabs on recent assignment submissions, and grade assignments. Students can view and turn in assignments and check their latest grades. Class discussions can be conducted securely, both during and outside of school hours.

It is customized for each particular school. Therefore this would be an app/program that the school administration would have to adopt for the entire school.

Price: Free

## Mobile Mouse

Mobile Mouse instantly transforms your iPhone or iPod touch into a wireless, multi-touch trackpad mouse.

(This one is a little tricky to set up. I needed to add my ip address.)

Price: $2.99

## Any.Do

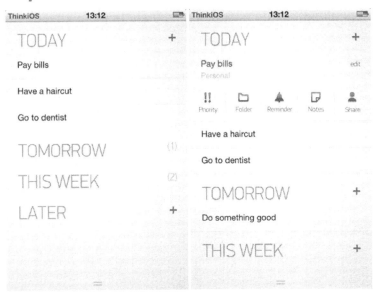

Millions of people use Any.Do every day to organize everything they do. With Any.Do you can easily capture all the things you want to do and make sure you get them done. It's free, simple, and fun.

Price: Free

## IEPPAL

IEPPal is an iPad-based data collection tool that enables general and special education professionals, in all disciplines to capture observed student event data.

Price: Free with an IEPPAL Subscription

## ShowMe Interactive Whiteboard by Easel

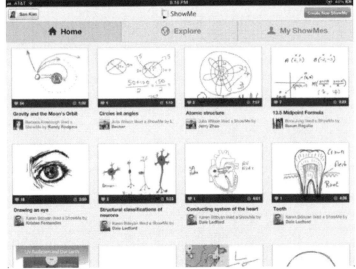

ShowMe allows you to record voice-over whiteboard tutorials and share them online.

This app is great for building tutorials. Students can make their own Khan Academy-style videos and post them online.

Price: Free

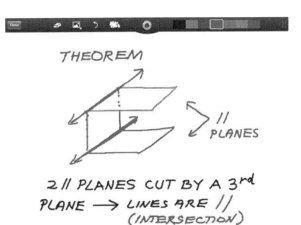

Android: Whiteboard by Henry Huang

Price: Free

## Educreations

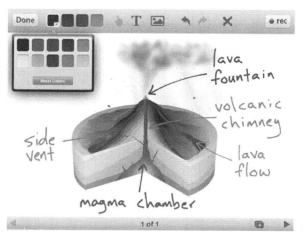 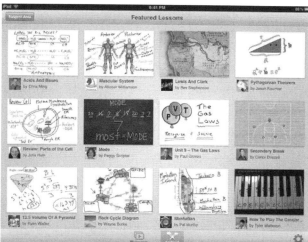

 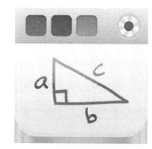 Educreations turns your iPad into a recordable whiteboard. Creating a great video tutorial is as simple as touching, tapping, and talking. Create animated lessons and add commentary to your photos.

Price: Free

## Haiku Deck

## Education Spotlight

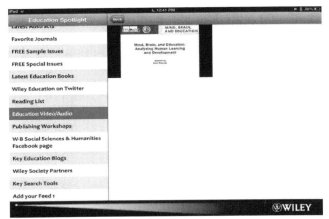

According to Wiley, "Education Spotlight is a must-have app for education researchers and educators."

Price: Free
That said, some functions such as journals, abstracts, and books won't work unless you have a login/subscription to a Wiley product.

## Pinterest

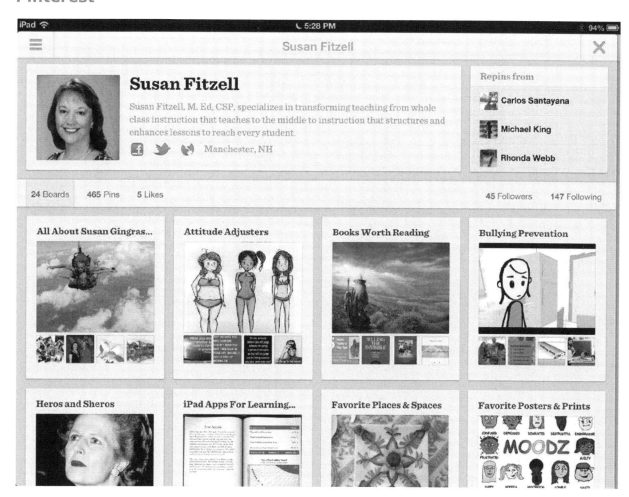

Price: Free

## Facebook

Price: Free

## Tech4Teachers

The purpose of this collection of apps is to equip teachers by sharing with them a collection of tools and internet resources to meet the educational needs of students in the 21st Century.

Price: Free

This is a compilation of all the portable apps we've researched for you listed *ALL* in one place!

www.SusanFitzell.com

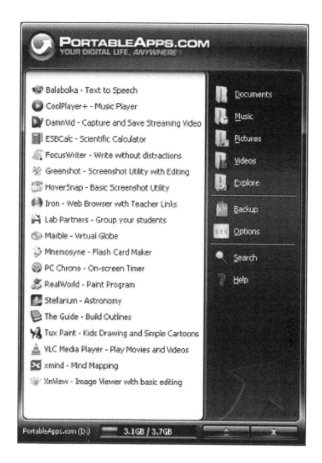

# Have fun!

I'm sure that by the time you read this book there will be countless additional apps for the iPad, Droid, and Windows 8 tablets. The one certain thing about technology is; it changes and it changes fast.

Exploring the different options available, sorting out those worth your, and your students', time and those that are junk can be time consuming. Learning new apps also requires time - some more than others. However, it truly is worth the effort when you find a piece of technology that increases productivity, achievement, or is simply brain engaging and fun.

If you are a technophobe, I encourage you to step out of your comfort zone and explore. Who knows what you might discover that would add value to your tech experience and life?

I never touched an iPad before I accepted the challenge to write this book and develop this seminar. Though I had some very frustrating moments (and occasional hours), I've found many apps to be extremely beneficial and the effort to be well worth the time.

Dive in!

## Bright Ideas

## Tech4Teachers USB Flash Drive!

One of the most common issues raised by teachers when discussing how to use technology has to do with their difficulties in finding, and installing, the software they need to support best-practice teaching strategies in their classrooms.

To support those teachers, we've researched a collection of free or open source, portable technology solutions that support the strategies that Susan Fitzell talks about most in her seminars and when coaching, and compiled them all on a single, easy-to-use USB flash drive. Every application and tool on this device is free or open source, portable, and as easy to use as possible. We use the PortableApps menu system to easily run these applications from a 2GB USB flash drive, so there is plenty of space left to customize and save files created with these tools.

As an extra bonus, the Iron web browser, included on the drive, is pre-configured with a selection of FREE websites and web-based tools that supplement or support the applications included on the drive!

To order, simply send this page with your payment or fax it with your PO to 603-218-6291. For bulk orders of 10 or more, please call us at 603-625-6087. For a complete list of application and tools included, visit www.SusanFitzell.com.

| Tech4Teachers USB Flash Drive | Quantity - _____ X $19.95 each = | |
|---|---|---|
| | Shipping and Handling (1-10 drives) | $4.95 |
| | Order Total | |

Please note: Orders with incomplete or incorrect information cannot be processed.
Customer Name:

_____

Address:_____

City, State Zip code: _____

Email address: _____

Phone number(s): _____

Payment Type: _____ Check _____ Credit _____ PO#_____

VISA/MC # _____ Expiration Date _____ / _____

Name on card: _____

## *Bright Ideas*

_____

_____

_____

_____

_____

_____

_____

_____

_____

_____

_____

_____

***For additional resources, visit www.SusanFitzell.com.***

Made in the USA
San Bernardino, CA
05 July 2013